PRINCEWILL LAGANG

Entrepreneur's Modern "The Modern Entrepreneur's Playbook

Contents

1

Introduction

In a world marked by constant change and innovation, entrepreneurship stands at the forefront of economic and societal progress. The journey of an entrepreneur is both thrilling and challenging, filled with opportunities and obstacles that demand creative thinking, resilience, and a strategic mindset. "The Modern Entrepreneur's Playbook" is a comprehensive guide designed to accompany you on this dynamic path, whether you're an aspiring entrepreneur embarking on your first venture or an experienced business owner seeking to enhance your entrepreneurial skills.

This playbook is a roadmap that covers a wide spectrum of topics crucial for entrepreneurial success. From developing the entrepreneurial mindset and generating viable business ideas to crafting robust business plans, navigating financial complexities, and leading high-performing teams, each chapter is a stepping stone in your entrepreneurial journey. Furthermore, it delves into the pressing issues of our time, such as social responsibility, sustainability, and adapting to the ever-changing landscape of entrepreneurship.

Each chapter is packed with valuable insights and practical advice, drawn from real-world experiences and the latest business trends. We believe that entrepreneurship is a continuous journey, not a destination. It's about embracing change, learning from successes and setbacks, and leaving a meaningful legacy for the future.

As you explore "The Modern Entrepreneur's Playbook," we encourage you to apply the knowledge and strategies to your unique entrepreneurial path. Whether your goal is to create a thriving business, make a positive impact on society, or build a lasting legacy, this playbook equips you with the tools, principles, and mindset required to navigate the challenges and seize the opportunities in the dynamic world of entrepreneurship.

The entrepreneurial journey is an adventure waiting to unfold, and we're here to guide you through its exciting twists and turns. So, let's embark on this journey together and unlock the potential within you to become a modern entrepreneur, shaping not only your own success but also the future of business and innovation.

2

The Modern Entrepreneur's Playbook

In today's rapidly evolving business landscape, the role of the entrepreneur has taken on new dimensions. Traditional business models are being disrupted, and innovation has become the currency of success. To navigate this dynamic environment and thrive as a modern entrepreneur, a new playbook is required—one that combines timeless principles with cutting-edge strategies. This chapter introduces "The Modern Entrepreneur's Playbook," a guide to help you master the art of entrepreneurship in the 21st century.

Section 1.1: The Entrepreneurial Revolution

The 21st century has witnessed a seismic shift in the world of entrepreneurship. With the advent of the digital age, the barriers to entry have been lowered, allowing more individuals to venture into the world of business. This revolution has given birth to a diverse range of entrepreneurs, from tech startups to socially conscious enterprises, all aiming to make a mark in their respective fields. In this section, we explore the evolution of entrepreneurship and why it's a remarkable time to be an entrepreneur.

Section 1.2: The Entrepreneurial Mindset

Being an entrepreneur is not just about starting a business; it's a mindset that permeates every aspect of life. In this section, we delve into the key components of the entrepreneurial mindset, including risk-taking, adaptability, creativity, and resilience. We also discuss the importance of embracing failure as a stepping stone to success and the ability to learn from one's mistakes.

Section 1.3: The Building Blocks of Success

Success in entrepreneurship is built upon a strong foundation. Here, we explore the fundamental building blocks that every entrepreneur should consider. These include:

1.3.1 Vision and Purpose
 - Defining your vision and purpose as an entrepreneur, and how these act as guiding stars for your journey.

1.3.2 Market Research and Idea Generation
 - The importance of conducting thorough market research to identify opportunities and generate innovative ideas.

1.3.3 Business Planning and Strategy
 - Developing a well-structured business plan and strategy to set the stage for your venture's success.

1.3.4 Networking and Team Building
 - Building a strong network of mentors, advisors, and collaborators, as well as assembling a dedicated and skilled team.

1.3.5 Financing and Funding
 - Exploring various funding options, from bootstrapping to seeking investors, and understanding the financial side of entrepreneurship.

Section 1.4: Technology and Innovation

In the modern entrepreneurial landscape, technology and innovation are at the heart of success. We delve into how technology is transforming industries, driving innovation, and offering new opportunities for entrepreneurs to disrupt traditional markets.

Section 1.5: The Role of Ethics and Social Responsibility

As businesses gain more influence and impact on society, there's an increasing need for entrepreneurs to consider ethical and social responsibilities. In this section, we discuss the importance of ethical decision-making, corporate social responsibility, and the role of the modern entrepreneur in contributing to a better world.

Section 1.6: Adapting to Change

Change is a constant in the world of entrepreneurship. This section explores the need for adaptability and the ability to pivot and change course when necessary. We discuss case studies of successful entrepreneurs who thrived by adapting to evolving circumstances.

Section 1.7: The Entrepreneur's Toolkit

To succeed in the modern world of entrepreneurship, you need a diverse set of skills and tools. In this section, we explore the essential tools and resources available to entrepreneurs, including digital marketing, data analytics, project management, and more.

Section 1.8: Your Personal Journey

Your entrepreneurial journey is unique, and your path to success may be different from others. In this final section of the chapter, we discuss the importance of self-awareness, setting personal goals, and staying true to your values as you embark on your entrepreneurial adventure.

As we embark on this journey through "The Modern Entrepreneur's Playbook," you'll discover the strategies and insights that can help you thrive in the dynamic world of entrepreneurship. Whether you're just starting your entrepreneurial journey or seeking to adapt and evolve in an ever-changing business landscape, this playbook will serve as your guide to success in the 21st century. Get ready to redefine the way you think about entrepreneurship and pave your path to a successful and fulfilling venture.

3

Ideation and Innovation

In the fast-paced world of modern entrepreneurship, ideas and innovation are the lifeblood of success. This chapter explores the critical process of ideation and the importance of fostering innovation in your entrepreneurial journey.

Section 2.1: The Art of Ideation

Ideation is the process of generating and developing new ideas. It's the first step in the entrepreneurial journey, and it sets the stage for everything that follows. In this section, we delve into the art of ideation, exploring techniques and strategies to stimulate creative thinking. We discuss brainstorming, problem-solving, and the role of inspiration in idea generation.

Section 2.2: Identifying Market Opportunities

An essential aspect of ideation is identifying market opportunities. It's not enough to have a great idea; you must ensure there's a demand for your product or service. We discuss market research, trend analysis, and the importance of understanding your target audience to pinpoint opportunities that align with your vision.

Section 2.3: Validation and Refinement

Once you have generated an idea and identified a market opportunity, the next step is validation and refinement. This section explores techniques for testing your ideas, obtaining feedback, and refining your concept to ensure it's viable and has the potential to succeed in the marketplace.

Section 2.4: Innovation as a Competitive Advantage

Innovation is a driving force in modern entrepreneurship. We explore how innovative thinking can provide a competitive advantage, disrupt industries, and lead to groundbreaking products and services. Case studies of innovative companies and entrepreneurs provide insights into how to leverage innovation to gain a foothold in your market.

Section 2.5: Building a Culture of Innovation

Innovation doesn't happen in isolation; it's a result of a culture that encourages and supports creativity. We discuss how to build a culture of innovation within your organization, fostering an environment where ideas are nurtured and innovation thrives.

Section 2.6: Overcoming Creative Blocks

Creative blocks are a common challenge in the entrepreneurial journey. This section explores techniques and strategies for overcoming creative obstacles, from battling self-doubt to dealing with setbacks. We'll also discuss the importance of persistence in the face of challenges.

Section 2.7: Collaborative Innovation

Innovation often flourishes through collaboration. We explore the power of teamwork, open innovation, and partnerships with other entrepreneurs, organizations, or research institutions to fuel creative and innovative endeavors.

Section 2.8: Sustainable Innovation

In the modern world, sustainable innovation is not just a trend; it's a necessity. We discuss the role of sustainability in entrepreneurship and how eco-conscious and socially responsible initiatives can drive innovation while making a positive impact on the world.

Section 2.9: The Lean Startup Approach

The Lean Startup methodology has gained popularity for its approach to entrepreneurship, emphasizing iterative development, testing, and learning. In this section, we explore the principles of the Lean Startup and how they can be applied to streamline the innovation process.

Section 2.10: Intellectual Property and Innovation Protection

Protecting your innovative ideas and creations is crucial in the entrepreneurial world. We discuss intellectual property rights, including patents, trademarks, and copyrights, and how to safeguard your innovations while navigating legal considerations.

Section 2.11: Case Studies in Ideation and Innovation

Throughout the chapter, we will examine real-world case studies of successful entrepreneurs who harnessed the power of ideation and innovation to bring their visions to life. These stories will provide practical insights and inspiration for your own entrepreneurial journey.

Ideation and innovation are the driving forces behind the success of many modern entrepreneurs. By mastering the art of generating and refining ideas and fostering a culture of innovation, you'll be better equipped to create products or services that meet the needs of your target market and lead your entrepreneurial venture to new heights. This chapter will equip you with the tools and knowledge needed to harness the power of innovation and turn your ideas into reality.

4

From Concept to Business

In Chapter 3 of "The Modern Entrepreneur's Playbook," we delve into the critical transition from a promising concept to a viable business. This chapter explores the practical steps and strategies that transform your entrepreneurial vision into a tangible and sustainable enterprise.

Section 3.1: The Business Model Canvas

The foundation of any successful business is a well-defined and flexible business model. We introduce the Business Model Canvas, a visual framework that helps you map out your business concept by considering key elements such as customer segments, value propositions, channels, revenue streams, and more. This section provides a practical guide to using the Business Model Canvas to refine and articulate your business idea.

Section 3.2: Prototyping and Minimum Viable Product (MVP)

Bringing your concept to life requires a prototype or a minimum viable product (MVP). We discuss the importance of prototyping and MVP development in validating your business idea, obtaining early feedback, and mitigating risks before investing significant resources.

Section 3.3: Market Entry Strategies

To turn your concept into a business, you need a well-thought-out market entry strategy. We explore various strategies, including market segmentation, pricing, distribution, and marketing, to ensure that your product or service reaches the right audience effectively.

Section 3.4: Scaling Your Business

Scaling is a critical phase in the growth of any business. This section discusses the different approaches to scaling, from gradual organic growth to aggressive expansion, and the challenges and opportunities that come with each. Case studies of successful scaling strategies are examined for insights.

Section 3.5: Business Legalities and Compliance

Starting and operating a business requires navigating various legal and regulatory requirements. We explore key legal considerations, such as business structure, permits, licenses, taxes, and intellectual property protection, to ensure your venture operates within the bounds of the law.

Section 3.6: Financial Planning and Funding

Effective financial planning is essential for the sustainability and growth of your business. This section discusses financial strategies, budgeting, forecasting, and the various sources of funding, from bootstrapping and loans to venture capital and crowdfunding, that can fuel your entrepreneurial journey.

Section 3.7: Managing Risks

Risk management is an integral part of building and operating a successful business. We discuss the identification and mitigation of various risks, including financial, operational, and market-related risks, to help you protect your business and make informed decisions.

Section 3.8: Customer Acquisition and Retention

Acquiring and retaining customers is the lifeblood of any business. We explore customer acquisition strategies, including digital marketing, social media, and content marketing, as well as the importance of customer relationship management and building brand loyalty.

Section 3.9: Business Culture and Team Building

A thriving business culture and a strong team are essential for long-term success. We discuss the development of a positive company culture and the strategies for recruiting, managing, and retaining a talented and motivated team.

Section 3.10: Measuring Success

To gauge the effectiveness of your entrepreneurial efforts, you need to establish key performance indicators (KPIs) and metrics for success. We explore how to measure and evaluate your business's performance, adapt to changing circumstances, and continuously improve.

Section 3.11: Sustainable Growth and Adaptation

In the dynamic world of modern entrepreneurship, adaptation is key to sustainable growth. We discuss the importance of staying agile, embracing change, and continuously innovating to remain relevant and competitive in the market.

Section 3.12: Case Studies in Business Development

Throughout this chapter, we'll examine real-world case studies of entrepreneurs who successfully transitioned from concept to business. These case studies will provide practical insights and inspiration to guide you in your own journey.

Chapter 3 is your roadmap for turning your entrepreneurial concept into a thriving and sustainable business. From refining your business model to managing risks, building a strong team, and measuring success, this chapter equips you with the knowledge and strategies to navigate the complex path from idea to execution.

5

Marketing and Branding in the Digital Age

In the fourth chapter of "The Modern Entrepreneur's Playbook," we explore the dynamic world of marketing and branding in the digital age. This chapter delves into the strategies and tactics that modern entrepreneurs need to build a strong brand and effectively reach their target audience in the digital landscape.

Section 4.1: The Digital Marketing Landscape

The digital marketing landscape is constantly evolving. In this section, we provide an overview of the digital marketing ecosystem, covering channels such as social media, content marketing, email marketing, pay-per-click advertising, and search engine optimization (SEO). We also discuss the importance of understanding your audience and leveraging data to make informed marketing decisions.

Section 4.2: Building a Brand Identity

A strong brand identity is a cornerstone of any successful business. We delve into the process of defining and creating a brand identity, including elements like brand values, mission statements, logos, color schemes, and voice. We discuss the importance of consistency in branding to establish a memorable and recognizable brand.

Section 4.3: Content Marketing and Storytelling

Content marketing and storytelling are powerful tools for engaging with your audience and conveying your brand's message. This section explores the art of storytelling, content creation, and how to use various content formats to connect with your customers and build brand loyalty.

Section 4.4: Social Media Strategy

Social media is a vital component of modern marketing. We discuss how to develop a comprehensive social media strategy, select the right platforms for your business, create engaging content, and measure the impact of your social media efforts.

Section 4.5: Search Engine Optimization (SEO)

SEO is crucial for improving your website's visibility in search engines. We explore the fundamentals of SEO, including keyword research, on-page optimization, link-building, and the latest SEO trends that can help your website rank higher in search results.

Section 4.6: Email Marketing and Automation

Email marketing remains a highly effective tool for reaching and nurturing your audience. We discuss email marketing best practices, list building, segmentation, and the use of marketing automation to deliver personalized and targeted content.

Section 4.7: Paid Advertising and Online Campaigns

Paid advertising, including pay-per-click (PPC) campaigns, is a valuable strategy for driving traffic and conversions. This section covers the principles of effective paid advertising, including ad targeting, bidding strategies, and measuring campaign success.

Section 4.8: Influencer Marketing

Influencer marketing leverages the reach and credibility of individuals in your industry or niche. We explore the benefits of influencer marketing, how to identify the right influencers, and the process of building successful partnerships.

Section 4.9: Analytics and Data-Driven Decision-Making

Data is a goldmine for modern marketers. We discuss the importance of data collection, analysis, and the use of analytics tools to make informed marketing decisions. We also delve into A/B testing and conversion rate optimization (CRO) to enhance the performance of your campaigns.

Section 4.10: Crisis Management and Reputation Building

In the digital age, reputation management is critical. We explore how to handle crises, negative publicity, and build a positive online reputation through transparency, responsiveness, and ethical practices.

Section 4.11: Emerging Trends in Digital Marketing

Digital marketing is a constantly evolving field. We discuss emerging trends in digital marketing, such as AI-driven marketing, voice search optimization, and the role of blockchain in digital advertising.

Section 4.12: Case Studies in Digital Marketing

Throughout the chapter, we'll examine real-world case studies of entrepreneurs who have harnessed digital marketing and branding strategies to achieve remarkable success. These case studies will provide practical insights and inspiration for your own entrepreneurial journey.

Chapter 4 equips you with the knowledge and tools necessary to navigate the ever-changing landscape of digital marketing and branding. Whether you're a seasoned entrepreneur or just starting out, this chapter will help you build a strong online presence, connect with your target audience, and create a memorable and impactful brand in the digital age.

6

Navigating Financial Management

In Chapter 5 of "The Modern Entrepreneur's Playbook," we delve into the crucial aspect of financial management. Sound financial practices are at the heart of every successful entrepreneurial venture. This chapter provides essential insights into managing your finances effectively and making informed decisions for the financial health of your business.

Section 5.1: Financial Planning and Budgeting

Financial planning and budgeting are foundational to your business's success. In this section, we explore the process of creating a comprehensive business plan, including setting financial goals, creating budgets, and projecting revenue and expenses.

Section 5.2: Accounting and Bookkeeping

Accurate accounting and bookkeeping are essential for tracking the financial performance of your business. We discuss the principles of accounting, setting up financial systems, and the importance of maintaining organized records.

Section 5.3: Financial Statements and Analysis

Understanding financial statements is critical to making informed decisions. We explain the key financial statements—income statements, balance sheets, and cash flow statements—and how to analyze them to gain insights into your business's financial health.

Section 5.4: Cash Flow Management

Cash flow is the lifeblood of your business. This section focuses on managing cash flow effectively, including strategies for improving cash flow, monitoring financial health, and dealing with cash flow challenges.

Section 5.5: Financing Options and Capital Acquisition

Access to capital is a pivotal factor for business growth. We explore various financing options, such as loans, venture capital, angel investors, and crowdfunding, and how to choose the right source of capital for your business.

Section 5.6: Cost Management and Expense Control

Controlling expenses is vital to maintaining profitability. This section covers strategies for cost management, including cost reduction, expense tracking, and the concept of lean operations.

Section 5.7: Financial Risk Management

Every business faces financial risks. We discuss the identification and mitigation of financial risks, as well as the use of insurance and contingency planning to protect your business from unexpected events.

Section 5.8: Tax Planning and Compliance

Understanding and managing taxes is a significant aspect of financial management. We explore tax planning strategies, compliance, and the importance of tax-efficient practices to reduce the tax burden on your business.

Section 5.9: Investment and Asset Management

Managing investments and assets wisely is essential for long-term financial success. We discuss strategies for investing in your business, diversifying investments, and optimizing your asset portfolio.

Section 5.10: Exit Strategies and Succession Planning

Planning for the future is crucial. This section explores exit strategies, such as selling the business, merging, or going public, as well as succession planning to ensure the smooth transition of your business to the next generation or a new owner.

Section 5.11: Ethical Financial Practices

Maintaining ethical financial practices is a core principle of a successful business. We discuss the importance of ethical decision-making, transparency, and corporate social responsibility in the financial realm.

Section 5.12: Case Studies in Financial Management

Throughout this chapter, we'll examine real-world case studies of entrepreneurs who effectively managed their finances and made sound financial decisions. These case studies provide practical insights and inspiration for your own financial management journey.

Chapter 5 equips you with the knowledge and skills necessary to navigate the complexities of financial management as an entrepreneur. Whether you're just starting your venture or seeking to optimize your financial practices, this chapter will help you make informed financial decisions, maintain fiscal responsibility, and achieve long-term financial success.

7

Growth Strategies and Market Expansion

In Chapter 6 of "The Modern Entrepreneur's Playbook," we explore the strategies and approaches for scaling and expanding your business. This chapter focuses on the techniques, challenges, and opportunities for achieving sustainable growth and market expansion.

Section 6.1: The Growth Mindset

Achieving significant growth requires a growth mindset. In this section, we delve into the importance of adopting a mindset that embraces change, challenges, and continuous improvement as you aim to expand your business.

Section 6.2: Market Research for Growth

Effective market research is vital for identifying growth opportunities and understanding your target audience's evolving needs. We discuss advanced market research techniques and tools to uncover unmet market demands and drive business expansion.

Section 6.3: Product and Service Expansion

Expanding your product or service offerings is a common growth strategy. We explore the process of diversifying your product line or entering new market segments, along with the associated challenges and considerations.

Section 6.4: Geographic Expansion

Expanding your business into new geographic markets can open up exciting opportunities. This section discusses internationalization strategies, market entry approaches, and considerations for global expansion.

Section 6.5: Strategic Partnerships and Alliances

Strategic partnerships and alliances can accelerate growth and expand your market reach. We explore the benefits of forming partnerships, how to identify suitable partners, and the strategies for successful collaboration.

Section 6.6: Mergers and Acquisitions

Mergers and acquisitions (M&A) are strategic growth options that require careful planning and execution. We discuss the intricacies of M&A, including due diligence, integration, and post-acquisition management.

Section 6.7: Franchising and Licensing

Franchising and licensing are strategies for rapid business expansion. We explore the differences between these approaches, how to franchise or license your business, and the legal considerations involved.

Section 6.8: E-commerce and Online Marketplaces

The digital age offers unique opportunities for growth through e-commerce and online marketplaces. We discuss strategies for establishing and growing your online presence, leveraging platforms like Amazon and eBay, and optimizing your digital sales channels.

Section 6.9: Innovation for Growth

Innovation remains a potent tool for driving growth. We explore how to foster a culture of innovation within your organization and harness innovative thinking to create new products, services, and markets.

Section 6.10: Managing Rapid Growth

Rapid growth can bring its own set of challenges. This section discusses how to manage and navigate the complexities of rapid business expansion, including scaling operations, securing funding, and maintaining quality and customer satisfaction.

Section 6.11: Risk Management in Growth

With growth comes increased risk. We discuss strategies for identifying and mitigating risks associated with business expansion, from financial risks to market-specific challenges.

Section 6.12: Case Studies in Growth and Expansion

Throughout this chapter, we'll examine real-world case studies of entrepreneurs who successfully scaled their businesses and expanded into new markets. These case studies provide practical insights and inspiration for your own growth journey.

Chapter 6 is your guide to achieving sustainable growth and market expansion in the ever-evolving entrepreneurial landscape. Whether you're aiming to expand your product line, enter new markets, or explore innovative growth strategies, this chapter will equip you with the knowledge and strategies needed to thrive in a dynamic and competitive business environment.

8

Leadership and Team Management

In Chapter 7 of "The Modern Entrepreneur's Playbook," we shift our focus to the critical aspects of leadership and team management. Effective leadership and building a high-performing team are essential for the success and growth of any business. This chapter explores the strategies, skills, and principles of leadership and team management in the entrepreneurial context.

Section 7.1: The Role of Leadership

Leadership is the cornerstone of a successful business. In this section, we discuss the fundamental principles of leadership, including setting a vision, leading by example, and the difference between management and leadership.

Section 7.2: Leadership Styles and Approaches

There are various leadership styles and approaches, and choosing the right one for your business is crucial. We explore leadership styles, such as transformational, servant, and adaptive leadership, and their applications in different business contexts.

Section 7.3: Effective Communication

Effective communication is central to successful leadership. We discuss the art of clear and open communication, active listening, and the ability to convey your vision, expectations, and goals to your team.

Section 7.4: Building and Leading High-Performing Teams

High-performing teams are the backbone of a successful business. We explore the strategies for team building, including team composition, roles and responsibilities, and creating a collaborative and motivating work environment.

Section 7.5: Team Motivation and Engagement

Motivated and engaged team members are more productive and innovative. We discuss techniques for team motivation, including recognizing and rewarding achievements, providing growth opportunities, and fostering a positive work culture.

Section 7.6: Conflict Resolution and Problem-Solving

Conflict is an inevitable part of any team. This section explores conflict resolution strategies and effective problem-solving techniques, including the importance of addressing issues promptly and constructively.

Section 7.7: Delegation and Empowerment

Effective delegation and empowerment are key to scaling your business. We discuss how to delegate tasks, entrust team members with responsibilities, and provide them with the autonomy to make decisions.

Section 7.8: Diversity and Inclusion in Leadership

Diversity and inclusion are increasingly important in leadership and team management. We explore the benefits of diverse teams, strategies for fostering inclusivity, and the role of conscious leadership in promoting diversity.

Section 7.9: Leadership Development and Self-Improvement

Leadership is a continuous journey of growth and self-improvement. We discuss leadership development, the importance of self-awareness, and the value of seeking mentorship and feedback.

Section 7.10: Remote and Virtual Team Management

In the digital age, remote and virtual teams are common. We discuss the unique challenges and opportunities of managing remote teams, including effective communication, tools for collaboration, and maintaining team cohesion.

Section 7.11: Succession Planning and Leadership Transition

Planning for leadership succession is vital for business continuity. We explore strategies for succession planning, identifying and nurturing future leaders within your organization.

Section 7.12: Case Studies in Leadership and Team Management

Throughout this chapter, we'll examine real-world case studies of entrepreneurs who have demonstrated exceptional leadership and team management skills. These case studies provide practical insights and inspiration for your own leadership and team management journey.

Chapter 7 equips you with the knowledge and strategies necessary to become an effective leader and build and manage high-performing teams in the dynamic entrepreneurial landscape. Whether you're leading a small startup or a growing enterprise, the principles of leadership and team management are critical for achieving long-term success.

9

Adaptation and Resilience in Entrepreneurship

In Chapter 8 of "The Modern Entrepreneur's Playbook," we delve into the critical subjects of adaptation and resilience. In the dynamic and unpredictable world of entrepreneurship, the ability to adapt to change and bounce back from setbacks is essential for long-term success. This chapter explores the strategies, mindset, and practices that will help you navigate challenges and thrive in the face of adversity.

Section 8.1: The Resilient Entrepreneur

Resilience is the capacity to endure, adapt, and emerge stronger from adversity. In this section, we discuss the characteristics of resilient entrepreneurs and how to cultivate resilience in the face of challenges.

Section 8.2: Embracing Change

Change is a constant in the entrepreneurial world. We explore the importance of embracing change, staying agile, and continuously innovating to remain relevant and competitive.

Section 8.3: Learning from Failure

Failure is a natural part of entrepreneurship. We discuss the significance of viewing failure as a learning opportunity and how to extract valuable lessons from setbacks.

Section 8.4: Adapting to Market Shifts

Market shifts and disruptions are common. We explore strategies for adapting to market changes, including diversifying your product or service offerings and seeking new opportunities.

Section 8.5: Crisis Management

Every entrepreneur faces crises at some point. We discuss crisis management strategies, including creating contingency plans, managing public relations, and leading your team through challenging times.

Section 8.6: Mental Health and Well-being

Entrepreneurship can take a toll on your mental health. We emphasize the importance of self-care, stress management, and seeking support to maintain your well-being in the face of adversity.

Section 8.7: Pivoting Your Business

Pivoting is the strategic shift of your business model or focus. We explore when and how to pivot your business, including identifying the right timing and approaches for successful pivots.

Section 8.8: Building a Resilient Team

A resilient team is an invaluable asset in overcoming challenges. We discuss strategies for building and leading a resilient team, fostering a supportive work environment, and maintaining team morale during difficult times.

Section 8.9: Legal and Regulatory Challenges

Navigating legal and regulatory challenges is an integral part of resilience. We explore how to address legal issues and regulatory compliance, as well as seeking legal counsel when needed.

Section 8.10: Leveraging Technology for Resilience

Technology can be a powerful tool for resilience. We discuss the role of technology in crisis management, market adaptation, and maintaining business continuity.

Section 8.11: Building a Safety Net

Preparation is key to resilience. We discuss the importance of building a financial and operational safety net to mitigate risks and ensure the sustainability of your business.

Section 8.12: Case Studies in Adaptation and Resilience

Throughout this chapter, we'll examine real-world case studies of entrepreneurs who have demonstrated exceptional adaptability and resilience in the face of challenges. These case studies provide practical insights and inspiration for your own journey in adaptation and resilience.

Chapter 8 equips you with the knowledge and strategies to navigate challenges, adapt to change, and build resilience in the entrepreneurial landscape. Whether you're facing a crisis, market shifts, or setbacks, the principles of adaptation and resilience will help you endure and thrive in the face of adversity, ensuring the long-term success of your business.

10

Social Responsibility and Sustainability in Entrepreneurship

In Chapter 9 of "The Modern Entrepreneur's Playbook," we explore the vital subjects of social responsibility and sustainability. As entrepreneurship evolves, the significance of ethical business practices, community engagement, and environmental consciousness has grown. This chapter delves into strategies, principles, and practices to help you build a socially responsible and sustainable business.

Section 9.1: The Role of Social Responsibility

Social responsibility is an ethical and moral obligation for businesses. In this section, we discuss the role of social responsibility in entrepreneurship, including the importance of making a positive impact on society and the environment.

Section 9.2: Ethical Business Practices

Ethical business practices are the foundation of social responsibility. We explore the principles of ethical conduct, transparency, fairness, and honesty in your business operations.

Section 9.3: Corporate Social Responsibility (CSR)

Corporate social responsibility involves actively contributing to the well-being of communities and society. We discuss the development of CSR programs, partnerships with nonprofits, and the integration of social causes into your business model.

Section 9.4: Environmental Sustainability

Sustainability is a growing concern in modern entrepreneurship. We explore strategies for reducing your environmental footprint, implementing eco-friendly practices, and adopting sustainable sourcing and production.

Section 9.5: Sustainable Supply Chain Management

A sustainable supply chain is a crucial part of your business's sustainability efforts. We discuss sustainable supply chain practices, including responsible sourcing, waste reduction, and supply chain transparency.

Section 9.6: Impact Investing

Impact investing combines financial returns with social and environmental benefits. We explore the concept of impact investing, the growth of the impact investing market, and how to align your business with impact investors.

Section 9.7: Community Engagement and Philanthropy

Engaging with the community and philanthropic efforts are essential for social responsibility. We discuss strategies for community involvement, corporate giving, and philanthropic initiatives that align with your business's values.

Section 9.8: Reporting and Accountability

Measuring and reporting on your social and environmental impact is critical for transparency and accountability. We explore reporting standards, such as the Global Reporting Initiative (GRI), and the importance of accountability to stakeholders.

Section 9.9: The Benefits of Social Responsibility

Social responsibility has numerous benefits for your business. We discuss the advantages of social responsibility, including improved brand reputation, customer loyalty, and attracting socially conscious consumers and employees.

Section 9.10: Social Responsibility as a Competitive Advantage

Social responsibility can be a competitive advantage. We explore how ethical and sustainable practices can differentiate your business in the marketplace and enhance your long-term success.

Section 9.11: Integrating Social Responsibility into Your Business Model

Integrating social responsibility into your business model is a holistic approach to sustainability. We discuss how to embed social and environmental values into your core business operations and decision-making.

Section 9.12: Case Studies in Social Responsibility and Sustainability

Throughout this chapter, we'll examine real-world case studies of entrepreneurs and businesses that have successfully integrated social responsibility and sustainability into their operations. These case studies provide practical insights and inspiration for your own journey in building a socially responsible and sustainable business.

Chapter 9 equips you with the knowledge and strategies to build a socially responsible and sustainable business. Whether you're starting a new venture or looking to enhance the social and environmental impact of your existing business, the principles of social responsibility and sustainability will help you create a positive and lasting legacy in the entrepreneurial world.

11

The Future of Entrepreneurship

In Chapter 10 of "The Modern Entrepreneur's Playbook," we explore the evolving landscape of entrepreneurship and the trends and challenges that will shape the future of the entrepreneurial journey. This chapter serves as a visionary guide to help you prepare for what's to come and thrive in an ever-changing world of business.

Section 10.1: The Entrepreneurial Ecosystem

The entrepreneurial ecosystem is evolving rapidly. In this section, we discuss the components of the modern entrepreneurial ecosystem, including incubators, accelerators, coworking spaces, and how they support and shape the entrepreneurial landscape.

Section 10.2: Emerging Technologies and Innovation

The future of entrepreneurship is intimately linked with emerging technologies. We explore the impact of technologies such as artificial intelligence, blockchain, biotechnology, and more on the business world and the opportunities they offer to innovative entrepreneurs.

Section 10.3: The Gig Economy and Freelancing

The gig economy and freelancing are transforming the way people work and start businesses. We discuss the implications of the gig economy, including the rise of remote work and the importance of adaptability for entrepreneurs.

Section 10.4: Social Entrepreneurship and Impact Businesses

Social entrepreneurship and impact businesses are gaining prominence. We explore the rise of socially conscious entrepreneurs who aim to make a positive impact on society and the environment while running profitable businesses.

Section 10.5: Globalization and Market Expansion

Globalization continues to influence entrepreneurship. We discuss the opportunities and challenges of expanding into international markets and how entrepreneurs can navigate a globalized business world.

Section 10.6: Regulatory and Ethical Challenges

As entrepreneurship evolves, new regulatory and ethical challenges arise. We discuss how to stay compliant with changing regulations and ethical standards in various industries.

Section 10.7: Entrepreneurial Diversity and Inclusivity

Diversity and inclusivity are essential for the future of entrepreneurship. We explore the importance of fostering diverse teams, supporting underrepresented entrepreneurs, and promoting inclusivity in the entrepreneurial ecosystem.

Section 10.8: Preparing for Uncertainty

The entrepreneurial journey is inherently uncertain. We discuss strategies for managing uncertainty, including scenario planning, risk assessment, and the ability to pivot in response to unexpected challenges.

Section 10.9: Lifelong Learning and Adaptability

Lifelong learning and adaptability are essential skills for the future. We explore the importance of continuous learning, upskilling, and staying adaptable in an ever-changing business environment.

Section 10.10: The Entrepreneur's Role in Shaping the Future

Entrepreneurs have a pivotal role in shaping the future. We discuss how entrepreneurs can influence and contribute to the future of business, innovation, and society.

Section 10.11: Preparing for Success

Preparing for success is as important as navigating challenges. We discuss the importance of goal setting, self-care, and maintaining a clear vision for your entrepreneurial journey.

Section 10.12: Case Studies in Future-Forward Entrepreneurship

Throughout this chapter, we'll examine real-world case studies of entrepreneurs who are pioneers in embracing future-forward trends and shaping the entrepreneurial landscape. These case studies provide practical insights and inspiration for your own journey in the ever-evolving world of entrepreneurship.

Chapter 10 serves as a roadmap to the future of entrepreneurship, helping you anticipate trends, challenges, and opportunities that lie ahead. Whether you're just starting your entrepreneurial journey or seeking to adapt and innovate in a rapidly changing landscape, the principles and insights in this chapter will empower you to thrive in the dynamic world of business.

12

Exit Strategies and Entrepreneurial Legacy

In Chapter 11 of "The Modern Entrepreneur's Playbook," we explore the important aspects of exit strategies and the legacy you leave as an entrepreneur. Preparing for the eventual exit of your business is as crucial as its creation, and understanding how to transition while preserving your entrepreneurial legacy is vital. This chapter provides guidance on planning your exit, succession, and the legacy you leave behind.

Section 11.1: The Importance of Exit Planning

Exit planning is often overlooked but is a fundamental aspect of entrepreneurship. In this section, we discuss why exit planning is essential, whether you plan to sell your business, retire, or transition to a new venture.

Section 11.2: Types of Exit Strategies

Various exit strategies are available to entrepreneurs. We explore the different types, including selling your business, passing it to a family member, merging with another company, or simply closing the doors.

Section 11.3: Valuing Your Business

Determining the value of your business is a critical step in the exit process. We discuss valuation methods, including financial metrics, market factors, and professional appraisals.

Section 11.4: Preparing Your Business for Sale

If selling your business is your exit strategy, preparation is key. We discuss how to enhance the value of your business, create a compelling sales package, and find the right buyer.

Section 11.5: Family Business Succession

Passing your business to the next generation requires careful planning. We explore succession strategies, including selecting the right family member, addressing potential conflicts, and ensuring a smooth transition.

Section 11.6: Mergers and Acquisitions (M&A)

Mergers and acquisitions can be complex exit strategies. We discuss the M&A process, due diligence, negotiation, and integration for a successful exit.

Section 11.7: Closing or Dissolving Your Business

Sometimes, closing or dissolving your business is the best option. We discuss the steps involved in an orderly business closure, including fulfilling obligations to stakeholders and complying with legal requirements.

Section 11.8: Legacy and Philanthropy

Your entrepreneurial legacy goes beyond your business. We explore how to create a legacy through philanthropy, giving back to the community, and supporting causes you are passionate about.

Section 11.9: Personal Transition and Retirement Planning

Planning for your personal transition and retirement is essential. We discuss strategies for financial planning, lifestyle adjustment, and finding purpose in the post-entrepreneurship phase.

Section 11.10: Entrepreneurial Mentorship and Giving Back

Entrepreneurial mentorship allows you to give back to the entrepreneurial community. We discuss the role of mentorship and how to be an effective mentor for aspiring entrepreneurs.

Section 11.11: Preserving Your Entrepreneurial Legacy

Preserving your entrepreneurial legacy is about ensuring your impact endures. We explore how to document your journey, share your experiences, and inspire future generations of entrepreneurs.

Section 11.12: Case Studies in Exit Strategies and Legacy Building

Throughout this chapter, we'll examine real-world case studies of entrepreneurs who have successfully navigated exit strategies and left a lasting entrepreneurial legacy. These case studies provide practical insights and inspiration for your own journey in planning your exit and legacy.

Chapter 11 equips you with the knowledge and strategies needed to plan your exit from your entrepreneurial venture and leave a meaningful legacy. Whether you're considering selling your business, passing it to the next generation, or exploring philanthropic opportunities, this chapter provides guidance on ensuring your entrepreneurial journey has a lasting and positive impact.

13

The Entrepreneur's Continuing Journey

I n the final chapter of "The Modern Entrepreneur's Playbook," we explore the ongoing journey of entrepreneurship and how it doesn't simply end but continues to evolve. This chapter serves as a guide to inspire and support your entrepreneurial journey as you continue to grow, learn, and adapt in the ever-changing business landscape.

Section 12.1: Lifelong Learning and Development

Lifelong learning is fundamental to your entrepreneurial journey. In this section, we discuss the importance of continuous education, skill development, and the pursuit of knowledge as an ongoing process.

Section 12.2: Innovation and Adaptation

Innovation and adaptation are vital for long-term success. We explore the importance of staying innovative, embracing change, and seeking opportunities for growth and evolution.

Section 12.3: Networking and Collaboration

Networking and collaboration remain essential. We discuss the role of building and maintaining relationships with fellow entrepreneurs, mentors, industry experts, and partners.

Section 12.4: Giving Back and Mentorship

Giving back to the entrepreneurial community is a way to share your knowledge and experiences. We explore the value of mentorship, providing guidance to emerging entrepreneurs, and supporting the growth of others.

Section 12.5: Balancing Entrepreneurship and Well-being

Balancing the demands of entrepreneurship with your well-being is a continuous challenge. We discuss strategies for maintaining a healthy work-life balance and ensuring your physical and mental well-being.

Section 12.6: Setting New Goals and Aspirations

As an entrepreneur, setting new goals and aspirations keeps you motivated. We explore the process of defining new objectives, challenging yourself, and working towards a vision for the future.

Section 12.7: Reflection and Self-Awareness

Reflecting on your journey and fostering self-awareness is a continuous process. We discuss the importance of introspection, learning from past experiences, and continuously growing as an individual.

Section 12.8: Embracing Change

Change is a constant in entrepreneurship. We explore how to embrace change, pivot when necessary, and adapt to new circumstances and opportunities.

Section 12.9: Fostering Resilience

Resilience is a trait that will serve you well throughout your entrepreneurial journey. We discuss how to continue building resilience, learning from setbacks, and bouncing back from challenges.

Section 12.10: Leaving a Lasting Legacy

Leaving a lasting legacy is an ongoing process. We discuss how to ensure that your entrepreneurial impact endures and continues to inspire future generations of entrepreneurs.

Section 12.11: The Entrepreneur's Pledge

In the final section, we invite you to make your own entrepreneurial pledge, setting forth your commitment to the principles and values that will guide your continuing journey as an entrepreneur.

Chapter 12 serves as a reminder that the entrepreneurial journey is an ongoing adventure. It provides guidance on how to embrace lifelong learning, innovation, well-being, and resilience as you continue to evolve, contribute, and make a lasting impact in the ever-changing landscape of entrepreneurship.

"The Modern Entrepreneur's Playbook" is a comprehensive guide that takes you on a journey through the world of entrepreneurship. Comprising 12 chapters, this playbook covers a wide range of essential topics, providing knowledge and insights for aspiring and experienced entrepreneurs alike.

Chapter 1: "The Modern Entrepreneur's Mindset" sets the stage by exploring the entrepreneurial mindset, motivation, and the skills needed to embark on an entrepreneurial journey.

Chapter 2: "Idea Generation and Validation" delves into the process of generating and validating business ideas, including market research, concept testing, and the evaluation of opportunities.

Chapter 3: "Business Planning and Strategy" guides you through the creation of a solid business plan, covering key elements such as market analysis, business models, and financial forecasting.

Chapter 4: "Marketing and Branding in the Digital Age" explores the dynamic world of digital marketing, including strategies for brand building, content marketing, SEO, and social media.

Chapter 5: "Navigating Financial Management" provides insights into financial planning, accounting, cash flow management, and investment strategies crucial for the financial health of your business.

Chapter 6: "Growth Strategies and Market Expansion" focuses on scaling your business through market research, product expansion, strategic partnerships, and innovation.

Chapter 7: "Leadership and Team Management" delves into the principles of effective leadership, team building, communication, and conflict resolution for creating high-performing teams.

Chapter 8: "Adaptation and Resilience in Entrepreneurship" emphasizes the importance of adaptability, resilience, and innovation in navigating challenges and uncertainties.

Chapter 9: "Social Responsibility and Sustainability in Entrepreneurship" explores ethical business practices, sustainability, and corporate social responsibility in building a socially responsible and sustainable business.

Chapter 10: "The Future of Entrepreneurship" offers a visionary look at emerging trends, technologies, and challenges shaping the entrepreneurial landscape.

Chapter 11: "Exit Strategies and Entrepreneurial Legacy" provides guidance on planning your business exit, succession, and the legacy you leave behind.

Chapter 12: "The Entrepreneur's Continuing Journey" underscores the on-going nature of entrepreneurship, emphasizing lifelong learning, innovation, and resilience.

Throughout the playbook, real-world case studies and practical insights help you apply the knowledge to your entrepreneurial journey. Whether you're a novice or seasoned entrepreneur, "The Modern Entrepreneur's Playbook" equips you with the tools, strategies, and mindset needed to thrive in the ever-evolving world of entrepreneurship and leave a lasting legacy.